ELEVATED **COCKTAILS**
Craft Bartending with Montanya Rum

By
Karen Hoskin

Cocktail Photography by
Nathan Bilow

Scenic Photography by
Matthew Berglund

ISBN: 978-1-4834-3492-6 (sc)
ISBN: 978-1-4834-3493-3 (hc)
ISBN: 978-1-4834-3491-9 (e)

Library of Congress Control Number: 2015910943

Lulu Publishing Services rev. date: 10/26/2015

For Brice Hoskin

For sipping happily
every cocktail
I have ever made,
and for sharing this
messy but wonderful
journey with me.

TABLE OF CONTENTS

FOREWORD

About four years ago, I traveled to Crested Butte, Colorado, to ride my mountain bike on one of the great trails of the world, the 401. After a particularly epic ride, I headed downtown and came across Montanya Distillers. Not expecting much, I stepped in for a cocktail, since craft cocktails are what I do for a living and are a personal passion of mine. I ordered the Maharaja Martini, and it absolutely blew me away. Over the remainder of my trip, I worked my way through the rest of Montanya's cocktail menu, most of which are Karen's creations, and have been incredibly inspired ever since.

I have been the beverage and entertainment director for The St. Julien Hotel in Boulder, Colorado, for 10 years. I work with my bar team to create the cocktail menus for our house bar, The T-Zero Lounge, and many events. On that trip to Crested Butte, my eyes were opened to how this local rum, distilled high in the Rockies, could play an intricate role, not only at the St. Julien, but also in the world of craft cocktails. Our customers have come to expect a Montanya Rum cocktail on our menu ever since.

In this book, on page 48, you will find one of The St. Julien's featured recipes for summer 2015, the Montanya de Oro, with a strawberry-basil shrub and a black pepper tincture. Enjoy!

Bryan Amaro
Beverage and Entertainment Director
St. Julien Hotel in Boulder, Colorado

COLLABORATION

A good cocktail recipe is a journey. Any bartender worth their salt knows that all cocktail recipes come to life after borrowing inspiration and cultivating ideas from other bartenders while learning, through trial and error, what works and what doesn't. It is a process of microscopic evolution, from inspiration to creation and revision.

To provide an example for how this process works, envision this: first, I enjoy a cocktail at a bar in New York or San Francisco that shifts my perspective ever so slightly. Then, I have a brainstorming session with a co-worker during a slow time at the rum bar. I notice an infusion someone made, so I grab it off the shelf to experiment. After creating that drink, it becomes a cocktail special. A customer gives me their thoughts on that drink, and again, I alter the recipe. It's a continuous cycle of evolution, collaboration and improvement.

The recipes in this book are the result of that evolution and collaboration at Montanya Distillers. Since I opened this bar in 2008, I have had the privilege and honor of working with a staff of nine incredibly talented bartenders. They not only serve; they create.

I tell our staff that Montanya's rum bar is their cocktail laboratory. For many years, I created several new recipes every week. Now I get more help from my colleagues. As a result, these recipes are a reflection of the creative laboratory in which we work every day. One of our bartenders calls it "Harry Potter-land for Grown Ups."

Thank you, especially to Delena Aseere Britnell, Lizzie Kost Loyer, Jodi Harper Nute and Robin Buza, for your impressive contributions to mixology at Montanya Distillers and to the cocktails in this book.

ABOUT MONTANYA DISTILLERS

Imagine fabricating something made out of your soul, every penny you possess and most of your waking hours. It might look a lot like our distillery. My husband Brice and I started the company in 2008 on a shoestring. Every day, when we make rum and then ship it off to far reaches of the world, like Singapore and New Hampshire, we are somewhat stunned. How have we come so far from those humble beginnings in Silverton, Colorado, in an 800-square-foot brothel?

Montanya Distillers has, from the beginning, been as much about rum cocktails as it is about making great rum. I have always loved creative rum cocktails. I landed my first bartending job in Bar Harbor, Maine, in 1985 and have been tending bar, in some way, ever since. Over the years, I would joke with my friends that I had a guaranteed invite to parties because of the inevitable concoctions I would make.

When I thrust myself into this career in 2008, I struggled to find decent rum cocktails, even in the best known bars. Bartenders would tell me year after year, "people don't drink rum." I would say, "But I do! Am I not people?" I am not sure which came first: the desire to make great rum, or the desire to make great rum cocktails for a crowd. They have always been inextricably linked.

My journey is not one most distillers take, but then, very little of what Montanya has done has been typical. Women distillers? Rum in the mountains? A bar that serves only rum? Montanya is all of those and so much more.

Almost daily, I am asked to publish a recipe book because so many travelers would like to drink our rum cocktails more often than they are able to visit my bar. I am happy and honored to oblige that request.

The recipes you'll find in this book are tried and true, tested on thousands of drinkers in our bar each year. That doesn't mean they are simple. Some are, many are not. If you run out of patience for the infusions and syrups, just start planning your next trip to Crested Butte, Colorado. We'll take care of you! Until you can come visit, I hope these recipes and spectacular photos from some of my favorite photographers will keep you inspired.

Oh Be Joyful Creek, Crested Butte, Colorado
Tributary water source for Montanya Rum

TEOCALLI

Martini glass or coupe

In a cocktail shaker with ice:

1/2 fresh lime, juiced
3 mint leaves - muddled in cocktail shaker
3 oz. Cucumber Infused Montanya Platino Rum (p. 50)
1.25 oz. Honey Lavender Syrup (p. 53)

Strain and serve.

Garnish with a floating cucumber wheel.

CALDERA

Follow recipe above.

In the shaker, add three slices of fresh jalapeño and muddle with the mint.

Garnish with a floating jalapeño slice.

MAHARAJA

This cocktail is an ode to my love for the flavors and aromas of India, and to my deep adoration for cocktails that balance spice with sweet so both can sing.

Martini glass or coupe
(option: rocks glass, top with soda)

In a cocktail shaker with ice:

1/2 fresh lime, juiced
1.5 oz. Maharaja Syrup (p. 52)
1.5 oz. Ginger Syrup (p. 53)
3 oz. Montanya Oro Rum

Shake vigorously. Strain and serve.

Garnish with a floating lime wheel and 3 Cardamom pods. Rim the glass with a combination of Turbinado sugar, powdered cinnamon and nutmeg (or other favorite spices).

BAY MANHATTAN

I have been obsessed with Italian bitters this year. This cocktail arose from my desire to tip my hat to the classic cocktails of old, while giving the recipe our typical Montanya twist. This cocktail has spoiled me, making every other Manhattan I try too sweet, too harsh or too syrupy.

Rocks glass or hi ball

In a crystal mixing glass:

2 oz. Montanya Oro Rum
1 oz. Carpano Antica Formula Vermouth
.5 oz. Bay Leaf Reduction (p. 51)

Place all ingredients in a mixing glass with ice. Stir with a bar spoon until chilled (do not shake). Strain into rocks glass over king cube.

Garnish with an Amarena or Luxardo cherry and a fresh bay leaf.

BERRY JIVE

Fresh berries and citrus make this cocktail irresistable on any day of the year, but especially on a sunny, summer day on a warm patio. The fresh basil and lemon tame the sweetness to make this cocktail light with just the right element of tartness.

Belgian beer glass

In a cocktail shaker with ice:

3 fresh strawberries
    (option: 2 fresh strawberries and 4 raspberries)
4 mint leaves
2 basil leaves
    (muddle ingredients above together)
Add:

.75 oz. Triple Syrup (p. 52)
2.5 oz. Montanya Platino Rum
1 oz. fresh squeezed orange juice
1 oz. fresh squeezed lemon juice

Fill glass with cocktail ice. Strain and pour over ice.

Garnish with a mint leaf and fresh berry.

The Castles, Gunnison Valley, Colorado

MOJITO

The downfall of the Mojito has always been sugar. I have sampled some Mojitos, even in cocktail bars I love, that invariably overwhelm me with sweetness. Too often, bartenders rely on pre-prepared Mojito mixes and bottled lime juices to avoid squeezing fresh lime, resulting in an acidic and syrupy cocktail. Many bartenders also muddle the mint to within an inch of its life, releasing a grassy, vegetal flavor that ruins the cocktail's fresh lightness. I would only ever make a Mojito with fresh lime, no matter how much the limes cost. Anything else is cheating.

Tall collins glass

In the empty glass, prepare the following:

1 fresh lime, juiced
2.5 oz. Montanya Platino Rum
.25 oz. Simple Syrup (p. 52)
6 - 8 mint leaves - lightly muddled in a mortar and pestle

Add cocktail ice. Stir with a bar spoon. Top with club soda or seltzer.

Garnish with half a Turbinado sugar rim and fresh mint.

Options: Add fresh muddled blackberry or raspberry for a twist! Or try muddled strawberry and replace the mint with basil for a truly unique "Bojito."

RUBY ROSE SALTY DOG

I have always been a fan of the Greyhound cocktail, but I can't drink vodka because of the excruciating headache I always get the next day. I wanted to create a Greyhound or Salty Dog-style Platino cocktail, but Robin really brought this concept alive with the addition of fresh rosemary and the fabulous zested rim.

Rocks glass

In a shaker with ice:

2.5 oz. Montanya Platino Rum
1/2 ruby red grapefruit, juiced
.25 oz. Simple Syrup (p. 52)
Small branch of fresh rosemary
Pinch of salt

Shake and strain over ice.

Garnish with a fresh rosemary sprig and a Turbinado, Kosher salt, and grapefruit zest rim.

SCARLETT O'HARA

The original Scarlett O'Hara cocktail was made with Southern Comfort, cranberry juice and lime. It never excited me very much, but I am a huge fan of anything with the authentic, dry taste of fresh cranberries. It made sense to reimagine this classic to fit my own tastes. It pairs beautifully with all your holiday dinners.

Champagne coupe

In a cocktail shaker with ice:

2.5 oz. Montanya Platino Rum
1 tsp. organic cranberry juice
 (use frozen concentrated form)
1/2 fresh lime, juiced

.25 oz. Simple Syrup (p. 52)
 (to taste, depending on the sweetness of the cranberry concentrate)

Shake and strain. Top with Champagne or Prosecco.

Garnish with a mixed sugar rim (organic, Turbinado and evaporated cane sugar are our favorites) and three fresh cranberries on a bamboo cocktail skewer.

FIERY PASSION

There is no cocktail flavor more unique and hard to find than passionfruit. For this cocktail, we use an organic purée imported from France. There is, sadly, no substitute. Many bartenders may order some type of passionfruit product for you from their bar suppliers. Don't be tempted to use a store-bought passionfruit juice.

Tall collins glass

In a shaker with ice:

2.5 oz. Habanero Pineapple Infused Platino (p. 51)
1 fresh lime, juiced
2 oz. juice made from passionfruit purée
.5 oz. light agave syrup
6 fresh mint leaves - lightly muddled

Shake and strain over ice. Top with club soda or seltzer.

Garnish with a half spiced sugar rim (Turbinado sugar, cinnamon and nutmeg), a fresh pineapple wedge and fresh mint sprig.

The Ruby Range of the Elk Mountains, near Crested Butte, Colorado
Tributary basin for Montanya Rum

WHITE ROOM

If you have ever been skiing on a powder day with the snow flying so intensely in your face that you can barely see, you have been in The White Room. I originally created this recipe for a friend's wedding, but I tried it on our regular menu soon after. When customers started calling ahead to order doubles, it quickly became known as a local's favorite - perfect after a cold, exhausting day of skiing the deep Colorado powder.

Martini glass or a tall collins glass

In a shaker with ice:

1.75 oz. Vanilla Infused Montanya Platino Rum (p. 50)
1.25 oz. Montanya Oro Rum
2 oz. half and half
.5 oz. Simple Syrup
.25 oz. Giffard Orgeat

Garnish with a pinch of almond bits, powdered cinnamon and a crushed almond rim.

KA TAO

Lemongrass, Kaffir lime and basil are sublime together and conjure up images of the long boats and island beaches of Thailand, of which Ka Tao is one of the most spectacular.

Rocks glass

In a shaker with ice:

1.5 oz. coconut water
.5 oz. coconut milk
.5 oz. agave syrup
1/2 fresh lime, juiced
2.5 oz. Thai Infused Montanya Platino Rum
3 fresh basil leaves, muddled

Shake and strain over ice. Top with 7 drops of Montanya Thai Bitters.

Garnish with fresh lime, fresh lemongrass, or fresh basil.

Thai Infusion
Zest of one lemon and one lime, 3/4 cup unsweetened coconut, 1 cup finely chopped fresh pineapple, 5 Kaffir lime leaves, 1 slice of jalapeño, 2 chunks of ginger root, .5 tsp. coriander powder, all in 1 bottle of Montanya Platino Rum. Infuse for 4 days. Strain and store indefinitely.

PIÑA COLADA

For most of my life, I thought Piña Coladas were blender drinks made with ice and cream. It wasn't until I began researching the history of the cocktail, which I was drinking on an island when I decided to start a rum distillery, that I realized how misunderstood this cocktail had long been in the United States. The addition of fresh lime and mint balances its elements and makes it accessible to those of us who cannot handle too much richness and sweetness.

Tall pilsner glass or martini glass

In a shaker with ice:

1.25 oz. Costamar Cream of Coconut
1.5 oz. organic pineapple juice
3 oz. Montanya Platino Rum
1/2 fresh lime, juiced

Shake vigorously. Strain over ice or into a martini glass.

Garnish with a pineapple wedge (on the rocks) or a floating lime wheel (in a martini glass), and a fresh mint sprig.

Matt Berglund

MOUNTAIN DAIQUIRI

The classic daiquiri, in all its forms, is my favorite cocktail on Earth. It is phenomenally simple, yet challenging to balance properly. It sits precipitously on the edge of being too strong or too limey. It begs for smooth spirits to allow the rum to shine. I love this interpretation of this cocktail because it features both Montanya rums, Platino and Oro. The dark rum adds a little more body than many recipes, and it represents our own unique, mountain tradition.

Rocks glass or champagne coupe

In a shaker with ice:

1/2 fresh lime, juiced
2 oz. Montanya Platino Rum
1 oz. Montanya Oro Rum
.5 oz. Simple Syrup (p. 52)

Shake and strain over ice or into a coupe.

Garnish with a lime twist, heavy lime peel, or lime wheel, and a combo Kosher salt and sugar rim.

The Slate River, Crested Butte, Colorado
Pure mountain water makes great cocktail ice, great ingredients and great spirits.

DARK MONK

It is rare to see a fresh fruit cocktail made strong with dark rum. I have been so inspired by the incredible Tiki cocktails that have seen a renaissance in this decade. This is by no means a Tiki cocktail, but the baking spices of the Snake Oil and the fresh fruit take their inspiration from that tradition.

Rocks glass or champagne coupe

In a shaker with ice:

3 blackberries (muddled)
2.5 oz. Montanya Oro Rum
.5 oz. Dr. Bob's Snake Oil (p. 51)
.75 oz. Honey Syrup (p. 53)
1 fresh lemon, juiced
3 dashes of Montanya Citrus Bitters (or any citrus bitter)

Shake and strain over ice (if using a rocks glass) or into a coupe.

Garnish with a fresh blackberry.

RUM OLD FASHIONED

I have never been a Bourbon or Rye fan, but I love the classics and bitters. I was sure this classic cocktail, reimagined with Montanya Oro Rum, would provide an alternative for others like me. Simplicity is a glorious thing, and this cocktail expresses classic simplicity more than most.

Rocks glass

Stack in the bottom of the empty glass:

A slice of fresh orange
1 Amarena or Luxardo cherry
Pinch of sugar
　　(Muddle together with a wooden cocktail muddler)

Add:

.25 oz. Simple Syrup (p. 52)
3 oz. Montanya Oro Rum
5 drops of Montanya Citrus Bitters
King ice cube

Stir with a bar spoon (do not shake) until chilled.

Garnish with an additional Amarena or Luxardo cherry.

RIO DE JANEIRO

Every rum bar must have a rich and decadent beach cocktail to assuage the craving of customers who will forever associate rum with the islands. We make mountain rum, but even I have my favorites from the beach.

Rocks or tall collins glass

In a shaker with ice:

3 oz. Montanya Oro Rum
1 oz. fresh pineapple juice
1/4 cup Costamar Cream of Coconut
1.5 oz. fresh squeezed orange juice

Shake and strain over ice. Drizzle with a dash of Grenadine. Sprinkle with nutmeg.

Garnish with an Amarena or Luxardo cherry.

PAINKILLER

2.5 oz. Montanya Oro Rum
2 oz. fresh pineapple juice
.5 oz. Costamar Cream of Coconut
1.5 oz. fresh squeezed orange juice

Follow instructions above.

Scott DW Smith

BASIL PARADISI

Martini glass or champagne coupe

In a shaker with ice:

1/2 fresh lime, juiced
2 oz. fresh grapefruit, juiced
.5 oz. Simple Syrup (p. 52
3 fresh basil leaves - muddled
3 oz. Basil Infused Platino (p. 51)

Shake and strain into a martini glass.

Garnish with a basil leaf.

Oliver Weinberg of The Kitchen Denver

MONTANYA RUM COCKTAILS
from some of my favorite bartenders

Oliver Weinberg's
Raddington

Champagne coupe

In a shaker with ice:

1.5 oz. Montanya Oro Rum
.5 oz. Lillet Blanc
.5 oz. fresh grapefruit juice
.5 oz. fresh orange juice
Leopold Bros Absinthe for rinsing

Shake in a cocktail shaker, not including the absinthe. Use a small bit of absinthe to rinse a coupe glass. Strain cocktail into coupe.

Garnish with a grapefruit swath.

Gold Fashioned

Rocks glass

2 oz. Montanya Oro Rum
1 sugar cube, soaked w/ Peychauds Bitters
    (approximately 4 dashes)
1/4 fresh grapefruit, juiced
King ice cube

Muddle sugar and grapefruit, add rum and stir.

Garnish with a grapefruit wedge.

MONTANYA RUM COCKTAILS
from some of my favorite bartenders

Andrew Amaro's
Montanya de Oro

Tall collins glass

In a shaker with ice:

2 oz. Montanya Oro
1.5 oz. Strawberry - Basil Shrub
1 oz. fresh pineapple juice
.5 oz. fresh lime juice
4 dashes of Cocktail Kingdom Wormwood Bitters
3 dashes of Black Pepper Tincture

Shake and strain all ingredients except Pepper Tincture over crushed ice. Drop 3 dashes of Black Pepper Tincture over top of the drink.

Garnish with fresh strawberry!

Strawberry-Basil Shrub

1 lb. of mashed strawberries
8.5 oz. natural sugar

Boil strawberries until white.
Add 1/2 cup fresh basil.
Boil 10-12 minutes and remove from heat.
Cool for 5 minutes and add
1/4 cup apple cider vinegar.

Black Pepper Tincture

Crack 6 whole peppercorns.
Infuse in 5 oz. of Montanya Platino Rum for 1 day.

INFUSIONS AND LIQUEURS

There are many ways to flavor a spirit and a cocktail. I am a purist about this process. I believe in flavoring spirits through natural, fresh ingredients soaked in rum. I particularly object to flavoring agents (natural or artifical) and chemicals like propylene glycol, which are fairly popular in flavored spirits. Making infusions is very easy, it just takes a little advanced planning. There is no need to refrigerate infusions, and they last indefinitely. However, with the exception of vanilla pods, I recommend removing any fruit, vegetables or herbs after four days to avoid over-infusing. Avoid including peels, especially when they have been cut open, as they will introduce a pithy flavor.

Cucumber Infusion
Peel one cucumber, remove seeds and chop into pieces. Infuse into 1 bottle of Montanya Platino for 4+ days. No need to refrigerate. Remove cucumber after 4 days.

Vanilla Infusion
Place 1 long pod of Madagascar Vanilla Bean into 1 bottle of Montanya Platino Rum. Infuse indefinitely.

INFUSIONS AND LIQUEURS

Habanero Pineapple Infusion
Take the rind off half of a fresh pineapple and chop into pieces. Slice 1/2 to 1 fresh habanero pepper, wearing gloves. Place into 1 bottle of Montanya Platino Rum. Add the habanero in stages if concerned about the infusion being too spicy. If it gets too spicy, add more Montanya Platino Rum.

Basil Infusion
Place 10 leaves of fresh basil into 1 bottle of Montanya Platino Rum. Infuse for 4 days. Remove basil leaves and store indefinitely.

Bay Leaf Reduction
10 fresh (or dried) bay leaves to each 1 cup of water. Bring to a boil, transfer to a glass jar and let sit for 5 days before using. Store indefinitely.

Dr. Bob's Snake Oil
Skewer 1 fresh lemon through with 1 Madagascar Vanilla Bean. Press 10 cloves into the flesh of one fresh orange. Decant 1 bottle of Montanya Platino Rum into a large 30+ oz. container. Add the fruit and 1/2 cup Turbinado sugar. Allow to infuse for 4-5 days, stirring occasionally.

COCKTAIL SYRUPS AND SPECIALTY INGREDIENTS

A trick I have learned: always use whole spices in cocktail syrups. Powdered spices, especially cinnamon, add viscosity to the syrup, causing it to have a slimey texture and to separate easily. All of these syrups may be refrigerated for up to 30 days unless otherwise noted.

Simple Syrup/Triple Syrup

Bring natural sugar and water to a boil at a ratio of 1:1. Refrigerate. For Triple, use a combination of sugar, agave, and honey (1 part) to water (1 part).

Maharaja Syrup

2 1/2 cups water, 2 1/2 cups natural or organic granulated sugar, 2 1/2 tbsp. whole cloves, 7 whole cinnamon sticks, 25 Cardamom pods, 2 1/2 tsp. whole black peppercorns. Break all spices into small pieces in a mortar and pestle (do not powder the spices or substitute a powdered version). Place all spices in a dry frying pan and toast until lightly smoking and fragrant (do not burn). Transfer to a sauce pan and add water and sugar. Bring to a boil and let simmer for 45 minutes. Transfer to a jar, refrigerate and chill for 2-3 days before straining off spices.

COCKTAIL SYRUPS AND SPECIALTY INGREDIENTS

Ginger Syrup

Fill a 40 oz. Vitamix or durable blender carafé with chopped (but not peeled), fresh ginger root. Add 1 3/4 cups fresh lemon juice, 1 3/4 cups Simple Syrup (recipe included in this section) and 6 fresh mint leaves. Blend until finely puréed. Strain through fine strainer or cheesecloth bag. Refrigerate for up to 15 days.

Honey Syrup

3 cups water, 1 cup raw honey. Bring water and honey to a light simmer, stirring often. Remove from heat. Refrigerate for up to 30 days.

Honey Lavender Syrup

3 cups water, 1 cup raw honey, 1/2 cup dried lavender blossoms. Bring water and honey to a light simmer, stirring often. Remove from heat. Add lavender blossoms and stir until mixed. Refrigerate for 2-4 days. Strain lavender blossoms and refrigerate for up to 30 days.

Cinnamon Syrup

3 cinnamon sticks (broken into fine pieces in a mortar and pestle), 3 cups natural or organic granulated sugar, 3 cups water. Bring all ingredients to a boil. Remove from heat. Strain and refrigerate for up to 30 days.

IDEAS FOR PAIRING RUM
COCKTAILS WITH APPETIZERS

Artisan Cheese Platter:
We select both local and international cheeses for this appetizer.
Beehive artisan cheese from Utah - espresso and lavender infused cheddar
Haystack mountain applewood smoked chèvre from Boulder
Cambozola, manchego, prosciutto
Calabrese and finnochiona salames
Artisan crackers and fresh fruit

Fried Ravioli
Handmade artisan ravioli, breaded and deep fried
A slice of fresh mozzarella
Sliced fresh garden tomato
Fresh basil
Balsamic reduction

Polenta Stackers
Organic polenta with red pepper
Caramelized onions
Fresh mozzarella
Roasted red peppers
Local microgreens

Bacon Wrapped Jalapeños
Fresh jalapeños, halved
Mixed cheese stuffing of Neufchatel, Cheddar, Parmesan
Wrapped in bacon and broiled

Tenderloin with Oro Rum Glaze
Marinated tenderloin with a glaze of Montanya Oro Rum, butter,
    molasses, shallots, garlic, cracked pepper

Butter Rum Scallops with Latkes
Handmade latkes topped with seared scallops and a butter rum glaze,
    butter, cracked pepper, Oro Rum, honey

At Tales of the Cocktail 2013

At Monyanya Distillers
in Crested Butte, Colorado

ABOUT THE AUTHOR

Karen Hoskin began bartending when she was 18 years old in a busy Maine tourist town. She has been making craft cocktails from her favorite spirit, aged rum, since her early years behind the bar. Her freshman dorm room was a speakeasy of sorts, with students popping in to see what cocktails she was experimenting with that day.

Karen's love affair with aged rum ratcheted up a notch on Baga Beach in Goa, India, where she was served her first taste of Old Monk Rum, a vestige of the British Raj. This rum, a navy style, was her early introduction to the depth and breadth of the rum category. For the next 25 years, she has sought out and tasted many different styles of rum and experimented with culinary flavors (which were exotic in cocktails at the time), such as chai spices, basil, lavender and jalapeño in her cocktail recipes.

In 2008, Karen opened the doors of her own rum bar, housed within her artisan rum distillery, Montanya Distillers, in Colorado. The decisions to create a rum bar and to make American craft aged rum were simultaneous. The rum bar, which has won a number of awards and distinctions such as "Best Aprés Adventure Bar" from Outside Magazine and "Top Aprés Ski Destination in North America" by Curbed Ski, has put Karen's mixology skills, and those of her bartending team, on the American craft cocktail map. Montanya's rums have won 19 Gold and Silver medals in international competitions.

One of the goals of Karen's cocktail program, for which she and her co-workers develop over 100 new recipes a year, is to encourage drinkers to think differently about rum and the cocktails made with it. She likes to nudge consumers out of their "rum and coke" comfort zones with paradigm-shifting rum cocktails like those in this book.

Many bartenders come into Karen's bar thinking customers "don't drink much rum," but they leave knowing this is not true. Customers flock to Montanya in droves because the cocktails are made with great rum, fresh ingredients and "out of the box" inspiration. If more bartenders give drinkers this potent combination, they will be rum cocktail converts for life.

Nathan Bilow

Matt Berglund

ABOUT THE PHOTOGRAPHERS

Nathan Bilow

In his 38 years as a professional photographer, Nathan Bilow (pronounced Na'tan) has traveled the world for commercial and editorial clients, with innumerable international publications throughout his career. Nathan's photography has been featured over 20 times on the cover of Crested Butte Magazine and he has published <u>Edge of Paradise</u> and <u>Seasons of Paradise</u>, photography books that display the changing of Crested Butte from the 1970s to the 1990s. With a lovely wife and two children, Nathan has more recently focused his work in his hometown of Crested Butte, Colorado, photographing families, weddings and scenery, although he still works for various clients around the globe. Nathan shot all the cocktail and food photos in this book with the exception of two, as noted. www.nathanbilowphotography.com

Matthew Berglund

Matt Berglund is an outdoor photographer born and raised in Crested Butte, Colorado. Exploring the Elk Mountains for the last 20 years has given him a strong love for the outdoors and allowed him to develop a unique perspective of the landscape. Armed with a camera, tripod and eye for the sublime, he ventures out into the woods. He goes deeper into the wilderness than many photographers, which allows him to capture rare and pristine perspectives. Matt took all the scenic photos in this book. www.itsaberglund.com